YOUl

YOUR BOOK IS YOUR BUSINESS CARD

THE ULTIMATE GUIDE TO WRITING, PUBLISHING & MARKETING YOUR OWN BOOK TO BUILD YOUR BUSINESS

MICHELLE PRINCE

ISBN: 978-0-9965021-8-4

TABLE OF CONTENTS

INTRODUCTION

As a self-publishing expert and founder of the "Book Bound" Workshop, I get a lot of questions about writing a book. It seems most people want to write a book, but the majority of people just don't know where to start. That's why I wrote this book to answer your most burning questions about book writing, the publishing process and how to leverage author status.

My whole life changed once I made the decision to tell my story…to write my book. My entire business of speaking, coaching, hosting seminars and providing Done-For-You publishing services exists simply because I chose to "step into my greatness." I chose to tell my story. If I can do this, you can too. ■

WRITING

WHY SHOULD YOU WRITE A BOOK?

There is more to writing a book than meets the eye. Most people, who have written books, and especially those who followed the formula I share with you in this book, did not set out to write a book because they were good writers or dreamed of becoming an author. In fact, most will tell you the exact opposite reason for deciding to write a book. Most discovered the power writing a book can have on their personal and professional lives by understanding how their author status could radically increase revenue streams and catapult their business to levels previously unimaginable. You see, writing a book is not about writing at all; it's about sharing your story.

YOUR STORY MATTERS

I firmly believe everyone has a story and every story matters. YOUR story matters! You have something to share with people, which will make a positive difference in their lives. You've been through things in your life, good or bad, where others could benefit from your experience. You've gained insight professionally or personally others could be interested in learning. It's your wisdom, which gives others the hope, "if he can do it, then so can I" or "if he can get through it, then I can get through it too." It's an opportunity to get your message in the hands of as many people as possible, to help as many people as possible. Writing a book is about making a difference. While making a difference is certainly important, it's also not the only reason to write a book.

INSTANT CREDIBILITY

When you become an author, you instantly become more credible in the eyes of your clients, prospects, family and friends. Ironically, this credibility typically occurs in their eyes before they even read your book. The fact you wrote a book elevates you to a new level and makes you the authority on your chosen topic. It's essential you leverage author status in your business and differentiate yourself from the competition.

YOU'RE THE EXPERT

We all want to work with the expert, the authority. When a prospect is considering doing business with you or your competitor he/she is looking for "the best." The prospect wants to know he/she can trust doing business with you, therefore credibility plays a crucial role in building your business. Many large companies spend millions of dollars on marketing for this very reason. They understand the power of perception and its ability to leverage your business. But you don't have to spend a ton of money to achieve the same results. You just have to write a book.

I have seen this happen in various areas of business from carpet cleaners, real estate agents to doctors, and more. The type of business doesn't matter, in order for the phenomenon to work.

So why does it work? As one of my mentors once said, "It really doesn't matter WHY it works…it just matters that it works." But, there is a reason why it works. Writing a book takes time and effort. Not many people do it, especially your competition, so instantly you stand out. People assume you must be the expert if you are capable and committed enough to follow through with writing a book. Along with that, you've proven the confidence to position yourself as the expert…and we all want to work with the expert!

KNOW, LIKE & TRUST

My friend Bob Burg says, "People do business with those they know, like and trust." This is a very true statement and it's your job to let your prospects and clients really know you, so they will in turn want to work with you. So, how do we do that? The greatest and easiest way for your clients to get to know, like and trust you is to know your story, and they get to know your story by reading your book. By sharing your story, no matter the topic, it gives your prospects the chance to connect with you on a deeper level, which will lead to more opportunities.

MORE OPPORTUNITIES

Writing a book will invariably attract more opportunities to you. Writing a book makes you the expert in the eyes of your clients, prospects and friends, so naturally you will attract more opportunities. More opportunities leads to more sales, more sales means more money. But, don't misunderstand this important point. DON'T write a book to make money… write in order to attract more opportunities, which will allow you to create more money.

LEVERAGE

Writing a book is about leverage. It's about taking what you already know, what you are already sharing with your clients, and putting it in a format to leverage author status. The benefits are endless when you are an author, but those benefits will not occur unless you know how to leverage author status. In the Marketing section of this book, I share with you specific ways you can instantly leverage author status to build you business.

WHAT DO YOU WANT?

Before you can fully leverage your author status, you have to know what you want—what's your end objective? Like a GPS, you have to program in your destination first, in order to get where you want to go. You have to have an end-goal, a compelling reason to write your book, so you can both drive and measure your success. The alternative is going around in circles and not knowing if you have yet arrived! So, ask yourself what you really want. Do you want explosive growth in your business? Do you want more credibility with your clients? What about being the "Go-To" authority in your niche? Perhaps you want to help more people, attract more opportunities or create multiple revenue streams - or maybe you simply want to make a difference. No matter what your motive is, you have to know it for yourself, in order to truly leverage all that being an author can do for you. You have to know what you want!

WHAT'S STOPPING YOU?

Just knowing what you want will not guarantee your ultimate success. After all, if just wanting something was enough to get you where you want to go, then you would have been there by now! You also need to be clear on what's holding you back. I've seen it time and time again where people know what they want, but deep down they simply don't believe they will get there. Our minds are so powerful, as Napoleon Hill once said, "what we believe, we tend to achieve." Belief affects all areas of your life—your business, your relationships, your finances and beyond. If your outlook is negative, you could be keeping yourself from achieving your dream. You have to look honestly at what are you telling yourself. What do you really believe about the likelihood of success, about becoming an author, about yourself? These are not easy things to be honest and self-aware about, but the first step to overcoming these negative beliefs is to identify what they are. What are you telling yourself?

WHAT'S YOUR STORY?

My mentor and past employer, Zig Ziglar said, "Man was designed for ACCOMPLISHMENT, engineered for SUCCESS and endowed with the SEEDS OF GREATNESS." I love this quote because it gives hope. It means everything we need to be successful is already inside of us! We already have our "seeds of greatness." We just need to water those seeds, in order to make the most impact. You see, your seeds of greatness are your story.

What's your story? What can you share with other people, which can make a difference in their lives? What special gifts or talents do you possess that other people value? What experiences have you been through in life (good or bad) which enable you to help those who are still experiencing those things? It could be divorce, abuse, parenthood, or building a business…

You see, writing a book is just about sharing

what you ALREADY know and putting it in a format that more people can digest. It's about putting your experiences, advice and expertise on paper and getting it into the hands of the most readers as possible to help as many people as possible. Bottom line, writing a book is about making a difference.

FINDING YOUR TOPIC

The #1 question I get from potential authors is "Where do I start?" With so many details in the publishing process it can seem like a daunting task to get started. It can seem even more overwhelming to pick a topic. That's where our training begins today....How To Find Your Topic.

There's no limit to the potential topics you could write about in a book but the trick is figuring out what the right topic is for you and for your audience. You have to write a book, which will benefit the reader, and a book you want to write; otherwise your chances of failure are very high.

I want to share a formula with you that is guaranteed to help you find the topic for your first book. If done correctly you should have topics for multiple books. Lets get started.

Grab a sheet of paper and make a T-chart. On the top-left side of the T, write the word "Passions". On the top-right side of the T write the word "Experiences."

Once you've created your T-chart, start thinking about the left-hand column, your passions. List as many things as possible, which you are passionate about. Things you love, things you enjoy doing, things which "light you up." Don't over think it and don't think of the exercise in terms of writing a book....yet! JUST think about what you enjoy doing.

To give you a better idea, I'll share a few of mine. I love the beach...it's a place where I'm totally at peace. I connect with the ocean in a way I can't even explain. So, the beach is the first thing on my list.

I'm also passionate about personal development and growth. I strive to be the BEST I can be. I thoroughly enjoy reading motivational books, attending seminars and being around other like-minded people who want more for their life.

I love PUGS! I have a Pug named Zoe and she's my baby girl. I'm obsessed with Pugs because, well, they really are the most awesome dogs in the world, right?

I'm passionate about making a difference, encouraging others to be their best.

You get the idea….

Okay, you should have at LEAST five things on your list by now.

Now, forget about your passions and focus on the right side of the page. Your experiences! What practical experience do you have? It doesn't have to be job related, but it could be. Your experiences include the things you've done throughout your life. Maybe you have experience as a mother, a sales person, a business owner or fighter pilot. Maybe you have experienced something difficult like abuse, bankruptcy, divorce or low self-esteem. These things may not have been enjoyable, but they are your experiences and belong on your list.

While making your list, focus on thinking of as many things as possible related to what you've experienced in life, good and bad.

A few of my experiences include working in sales, being a Mom, dancing in my younger years, working for Zig Ziglar, writing a book, etc.

What about you? Make sure you get at least five things on your list.

Now, here's where the fun part comes! This formula is exactly how thousands of other authors discovered their book topic, and you will too.

Look at both your lists and see where you can find a connection, a similarity. Literally draw a line from one side of the T to the other side trying to link up similarities.

As you remember, one of my passions is personal growth and one of my experiences is working for Zig Ziglar. Do you see the connection? I'm passionate about personal development and being my best self, PLUS I've worked for the MASTER of personal development and have experience applying his strategies to my own life. A natural book topic would be a book about my experiences using the strategies I learned from Zig Ziglar, describing the ups and downs of life and sharing those experiences with the reader.

In my first book, "Winning In Life Now", which later became a best seller in two categories that is exactly what I did! Not to mention, the book was incredibly easy to write. It literally FLEW OUT OF ME and on to paper in under three weeks. No kidding!

Now is your turn to give it a try. Where do you see a connection? If you do this right, you will likely see MANY connections and MANY possible book ideas. If you have more than one, the easiest way to pick your first book topic is to see which one of those topics speaks to you the most and/or which would be easiest for you to write.

The reason passion and experience (and the intersection of the two) are so critical is without one or the other, you book project is doomed to fail. If you write a book about something you're passionate about, but have no experience, your book will lack depth or credibility. If you write a book about something in which you have experience, but no passion, you won't have the motivation to finish the book. It has to be an intersection between the two in order to write a book a reader wants to READ and a book you WANT to write. ■

PUBLISHING

Most people think if they just know the publishing process writing a book will be easy. The truth is, it can be easy, but only once you get your book out of your head and on to paper. But, before you can get it on to paper, you have to know what it is that you want to say. Essentially, the first step in the publishing process is not publishing at all. It begins with prewriting.

PREWRITING

Prewriting starts long before you're actually READY to write. It's never too early to begin capturing ideas, quotes, and stories for your book. Begin by keeping a journal of anything that comes to mind related to your book. Keep these stories in one place and don't worry about grammar, punctuation or any of the finer details at this stage, just jot down thoughts as they come. When you are ready for the drafting stage, these notes will be your guide to building your book outline.

Whether you journal in a notebook or write online, it doesn't make a difference in the pre-writing stage. All that matters is you take what's floating around in your head and capture these ideas in order to turn them into content.

Now that you have your story, it's time to figure out what to do with it.

OUT OF YOUR HEAD AND ONTO PAPER

Let's dive into some proven strategies to make sense of all those thoughts and ideas swirling around in your head! We're going to outline, step by step exactly how to get your story out of your head and onto paper!

Once the topic is identified, you'd think it would be smooth sailing getting the book underway, but this is where many would-be-authors fail. They don't have the tools to take the knowledge, expertise, stories and advice out of their head and get it onto paper. For starters, they don't know how to create the outline, which will eventually become their book.

Like most authors, I also struggled until I discovered a foolproof way to easily map out the contents of any book. I will detail precisely this method.

First, go back to the "Finding Your Topic" exercise. You should have a list of several possible topics, one of which you must select for the topic of your first book. Note, first book because this process often lends itself to creating authors of multiple books and I'm living proof!

Which topic jumps out at you? Which topic would be easy for you to get onto paper? Which topic do you find yourself talking about most frequently? The best first book to write should be the easiest book for you to write. Meaning, you don't need to do a lot of research to, you're your message across. It should be a topic you know well (for example, your life story) and it's one you should be able to get out of your head and onto paper pretty quickly.

Got a topic? Great! It's time to gather all the information you already know about this topic and get it onto paper in the form of an outline.

How is this achieved? There are many different ways, but I have found mind mapping to the most effective method of creating a book outline. A mind map is a diagram used to visually outline information. A mind map is often created around a single word or text, placed in the center, to which associated ideas, words and concepts are added. Major categories radiate from a center, and lesser categories are sub-branches of larger branches. Categories can represent words, ideas, tasks, or other items related to a central key word or idea.

Mind maps can be drawn by hand, or completed via online versions available on the Internet. Personally, I prefer drawing mine by hand. The outcome of this map, specific to writing a book, is creating an outline of all of your chapters, subchapters and stories to share within chapters. Seeing all your thoughts and ideas on paper is such an exciting first step and is accomplished in a simple and easy-to-understand way. In my "Book Bound" workshop, soon-to-be authors are guided through the mind-mapping process step-by-step to create their first book outline. Thousands of authors have already followed this formula and successfully created their book outline in less than 60 minutes!

BEST METHOD TO WRITE

Once your book outline is complete the next step is deciding which method will be best to get those thoughts on paper. Here are three ways to accomplish this and it's up to you to figure out which method is right for you:

1. Good ole fashion paper and pen—some love to write by hand, whether it is in notebooks, journals, on napkins, etc. If you can express yourself best in this way then by all means, do it! Get a journal or a folder and start writing down ideas as they come. You may get an inspiration for a story to share in the book. Get it on paper! There will be times when you have the motivation to write an entire chapter in one sitting and other times you will only write a sentence. The key to being successful with the paper and pen method of writing is to simply get it on paper.

   Now, of course there is an obvious downside to writing your book by hand. At some point, once you've proofed your work and are ready for an editor to review it, you'll have to get your written word into a digital format, most commonly a Word document. This is an extra step in the process, but if your creativity flows best with paper and pen then stick to your instincts.

2. The second way to get your story out of your head and onto paper is by typing your story. This eliminates the extra step of converting the written word into a digital format. Writing your thoughts and stories in a Word document from the get-go will greatly expedite the process.

Many of you, like myself, think best when you're typing on a keyboard. The creative juices start flowing as soon as your fingers touch the keys. If this is the case for you, again stick to what you know. In addition, it is definitely the simplest and most time efficient method.

3. The third and most common way to get

your story out of your head is to "talk" your book. By "talk" your book, I mean record yourself "telling" your story chapter by chapter. Your audio recordings can be sent to a transcriber who can convert your spoken words into a Word document, which in turn becomes your book outline.

There are many recording devices on the market today, so there's no need to overcomplicate. A digital recorder can be purchased, which will record your voice and download the audio files to your computer. You can even use a conference line to record yourself or simply make use of your smart phone. Furthermore, there are dozens of voice recognition Apps available for the same purpose. The bottom line is get talking and hit the record button.

DRAFTING

Once you decide your best method for getting your story onto paper, it's time for the "brain dump." The "brain dump" requires you to write/type/speak everything you know about your topic until it's all out of your head. As this is the drafting phase of the publishing process, not the editing stage, it's extremely important you do not critique your work just yet. Don't go back and reread your material until absolutely everything is out of your head. The goal is to allow your creativity to flow easily, so your thoughts can come out without disruption or killing your train of thought.

You must be disciplined in this stage. It is very easy to write a paragraph and immediately go back to re-read what you've written. Typically, if you don't like what you've written you may start rewriting, second-guessing and creating doubt. This is the point where many authors give up. They don't believe they have "what it takes" to be a writer, or it's too hard to get it out of their head, so they give up. Don't fall into the same trap and complicate the process! Trust the "brain dump" and you'll see your book come to life quicker than you could ever imagine.

PROOFING

At this point you've either written, typed or "talked" your book. Now it's time for you to proof, revise and ensure the content is contingent with your topic. It is your responsibility to thoroughly revise and proof your work BEFORE you hire an editor. Doing so will save you a lot of time and money.

Once you start the editing process, most authors are ready to put down their pen and be done with the whole thing. However, editing is the most important part of the book writing process! It's definitely not the most enjoyable part, but it is necessary to get your book exactly how you want it. Don't cut corners and think you're done…the fun is just beginning.

EDITOR

Once you've done your own proof reading and made sure all the details and content necessary are included, it's time to hire an editor. Hiring a professional editor is the best money you will spend in the publishing process. Once your book is published, it's out there FOREVER so you want to make sure it is done properly.

There are various levels of editing, as well as different types of editors, so it is important to do research to find the appropriate editor. Look for an editor who has edited books in your genre and can readily provide references. Before moving forward with an editor, make sure to negotiate rates and sign a contract with a specific timeline.

Your book will truly come to life once an editor has reviewed and made suggestions to your manuscript. Editors can be very talented and effective in making your story read well. Personally, I have found them to be invaluable in my book-writing process.

Your number one priority is for your manuscript to capture your story and be told in a way, which will help other people. It may take more time than you'd like, but in the final product will be something you can be proud of. Never forsake quality for speed. Spend the time perfecting your story before you take your book to print. ■

MARKETING

You have your topic and understand what to do with it, therefore it's time to start leveraging author status and monetize your message.

When you're an author, you IMMEDIATE-LY become more credible in the eyes of your clients, colleagues, family and friends. Even before somebody reads the content of your book, you are considered an authority just because you authored a book.

You also become somewhat of a celebrity, particularly in your local community, network and industry. You are now the go-to person on your subject. You are the niche expert on your topic. Now think, who loves celebrities and people of authority? The Media, which is the first way you can leverage author status to grow your business…and your bottom line.

MEDIA

Being an author will get you media attention! We all want to learn from the expert, but what does that mean for you as an author? Access to the media.

The media NEEDS authors, like you, to be credible guests on their shows and in their newspapers or other publications. When you are an author, you are considered "talk show worthy." You will be in high demand as an author because all TV, Radio, Newspaper, Magazine and other publication executives need guests EVERY SINGLE DAY! Their job is to bring value to the local community by talking to the expert. And who is the expert? An author is the expert…YOU are the expert.

You make their job easier, meaning they love working with authors.

For example, let's say you're a dentist and

you've written a book on everything you need to know before hiring a dentist. Your local media will likely hear about this and want to bring you on to the local news channel to discuss the importance of finding the right dentist. This kind of exposure is priceless and will radically impact your business by giving the public direct access to you, which in turn will bring you more leads and ultimately more opportunities. Sure, you can pay for media exposure, but authors don't need to because ultimately the media needs YOU!

PRESS RELEASES

So, how do we get in front of the media? Press Releases!

A press release is the easiest and fastest way to get the attention of the media. Press releases alert the media in your local community (or even around the country) you are a credible and newsworthy authority.

As an author, you can send press releases for

many different reasons. Send a release when you begin writing your book; send another release when the book is complete and yet another when your book is officially launched. The point is you want to keep the media up-to-date, so the local news outlets recognize you as a go-to-resource in your community. Once they become aware, you will be booked for radio interviews, TV segments, newspaper articles, etc. But, you can't get on the radio or TV or in the news if the media doesn't know about you. It's your job to get the word out with publicity and press releases.

This media attention and exposure will invariably get you more leads! More leads mean more opportunities, more opportunities leads to more sales. It's a beautiful thing!

Once you get a lead, it is important to keep them and convert them to a customer. A great way to do this is to give your book away for free!

YOUR BOOK IS YOUR BUSINESS CARD

Your book is the greatest business card you will ever own. People will throw away a business card, but they will not throw away a book. If you want to increase your leads, get your book in the hands of as many people as possible and give it away as a bonus. It may cost you a few dollars, but it's the best marketing investment you can make. When a prospect is considering doing business with you or with your competitor and he/she has a copy of your book, he/she will likely perceive you as more credible. They will perceive you as the expert...and don't we all want to work with the expert? Of course we do!

REFERRALS

Business 101 is understanding that people do business with those they know, like and trust. The best way for your clients to get to know, like and trust you is to read your story. But, it goes even further. When your clients know, like and trust you…they will tell their friends! Referrals are a great way to grow your business and having a book makes it exponentially easier. People don't typically throw away books, but what do they typically do with a good book? They pass it along. People pass around things of value. If you write about something you know and which will help other people, it is going to get passed around and will bring you referral business.

SPEAKING

Being an author, no matter your topic, will bring you media attention, more leads and referrals. It will also bring you speaking opportunities.

Even if you have no desire to be a professional speaker, speaking will allow you to showcase your book, your story and your business to more people in a shorter amount of time. You are selling one-to-many instead of selling one-to-one.

Like the media, companies, associations and groups want a speaker who is the expert and by now, you are the expert! Do not underestimate the power of speaking…it can exponentially explode opportunities for you as an author!

Personally, speaking has catapulted my business. If done correctly, this key step can make a dramatic difference to your bottom line. In my "Book Bound" workshop I share specific ways you can book speaking engagements in your local community, in order to start talking about your book and your business.

MULTIPLE REVENUE STREAMS

The #1 question related to book writing is "How much money can I really make as an author?"

Let's look at some simple math. Think of how much money you want to make this year. Is it $50,000, $500,000, $1Million? To keep it simple, let's use $100,000 as an example and follow this equation:

Number of Books x Book Profit = Revenue

Let's say you sell your book for $20. Now divided by your revenue target of $100,000, you'd need to sell AT LEAST 5000 books. Wow! That is a lot of books!

But actually it's even more than 5,000 because you won't net $20 per book. Considering the cost to produce the book, a more realistic profit is $10 per book. Therefore, you would need to sell 10,000 books to make $100,000!

How long do you think it will take you to sell 10,000 books? Probably a LONG time! But, there is an easier way to make money with your book by creating Multiple Revenue Streams.

People do not value books; they value the content found in books. So, a book is really just a vehicle to get your valuable content to your target market. By repurposing your content in multiple ways, it will give you multiple revenue streams. Here are seven potential opportunities to monetize your message:

1. Physical Book - Some people prefer to hold a book or put it on their bookshelf
2. eBook - Kindle / Nook
3. CD - Listening in the Car, Downloading to a device
4. DVD – Some people like to watch on their computer or DVD player
5. Seminar - Live Events
6. Home Study Course – A virtual version of the seminar
7. One-on-one Coaching - Direct access to you…the EXPERT!

All of these options utilize the same information. You're simply preparing the information in different ways, in order to target all demographics and learning styles, while also creating multiple revenue streams!

In my "Book Bound" workshop, I share more specific ways to leverage the concept of multiple revenue streams, as I see it as one of the fastest and most effective ways to monetize your message.

PRESELL YOUR BOOK

The bottom line in successfully leveraging author status and profiting from your experience is to differentiate and stand out from your competition. When you write a book and become the authority in that market, you no longer have to compete on price; you compete on credibility, which makes price a non-issue. In the mind of your prospect, because you took the time, had the courage and expertise to write a book, then you MUST be the BEST! Clearly, we already established we all want to work with the BEST!

The fastest and easiest way to make money as an author BEFORE your book is even written is through pre-selling. Once the manuscript is in process and you are within three months of printing, start selling your book at a special rate. Give your readers the opportunity to be the first to get your book and use the sales of those books to pay for publication costs. It is important to maintain your integrity and only pre-sell if you are committed to completing your book and can give readers an estimated ship date.

These are just a FEW of the incredible marketing strategies taught at the "Book Bound" workshop and I guarantee they will work, if YOU work. ■

WHAT'S NEXT?

I truly hope you are able to use these strategies to achieve your book writing goals. In my experience, however, just learning and reading the material is only the first step. It's a great start, but if you want to succeed, your actions are all that count.

Let's recap. We started by learning the techniques to finding your topic. It's simple: your passions PLUS your experiences equals a book you want to write and a book readers want to read. Make sure you complete the suggested exercise on narrowing down which book will be your best first book, in order to truly be successful in this stage.

Next, we uncovered three specific ways to get

your book "out of your head" and onto paper. Commit to one of these methods as quickly as possible and continue with your chosen method until you've done your FULL "brain dump". Remember don't edit at this point... just get it out of your head.

Finally, you learned how to leverage author status and monetize your message. Remember, no one will know about you or your book if you don't become a master at making others aware of your book and author status. You have to put the material into practice. Not just listen to it, not just talk about it, and not just think about it, but actually do it.

Beware of the little voice in your head saying something like "who are you to write a book?", "what do you have to say?", "you don't have time to write a book!" Notice who's doing the talking here, the conditioned mind, that's who! Remember, only you can keep you in your comfort zone. If you were comfortable with becoming an author, you would have done it by now. Do the writing, work the plan and see your life and your business explode!

I learned my way to success as an author and business owner, so now it's my turn to assist others. My mission is to motivate, inspire and encourage others to find their passion, live their purpose and share their story to make a difference in other people's lives. I know we all have a story and your story matters!

MY INVITATION TO YOU

I'm truly blessed to have seminars, workshops and programs, which transform people's lives quickly and permanently. I'm thrilled to have been able to help thousands of people become authors. From my heart to yours, I invite you to attend the three-day "Book Bound" workshop. This event will take you to an entirely new level of success personally and professionally. This event is where we actually create your book blueprint right on the spot!

In one incredible weekend you will break through whatever is holding you back from stepping into your greatness and sharing your story. You will walk out of the program with a brand new outlook on life, your strengths, your message, your purpose and yourself. Many attendees count the "Book Bound" workshop as one of the most important experiences of their life. It's fun, it's exciting and it's packed with profound knowledge and essential book writing formulas, which will guarantee your success. You will meet many like-minded people from all over the world, many of whom could be business associates and life-long friends. This is so crucial for you to attend that, for a limited time, I'm offering the workshop at a reduced rate with a 100% money-back guarantee. If you are not 100% ecstatic by what you learn on the first day, then we will refund your investment, no questions asked. That's right, it's guaranteed so you have nothing to lose and everything to gain. All the details are at www.BookBound-Workshop.com.

I believe you will step into your greatness and make a difference in this world! I believe you can do this! It's your time so take action now! Thank you for spending your precious time with me. I wish you tremendous success and true happiness, and I look forward to meeting you in person soon and I can't wait to read your book! ▪

.

For more information on Michelle Prince's speaking, seminars, coaching and Done-For-You Publishing Services go to www.MichellePrince.com or call 972-529-9743. Inquiries can also be sent to Support@MichellePrince.com

Michelle Prince is a passionate, dynamic speaker who captivates audiences with her authenticity, high energy and natural ability to connect with any audience. Michelle mixes enthusiasm, passion and humor with motivational stories to inspire others to start "Winning In Life"...and to do it NOW!

Michelle Prince is the best-selling author of her first book, "Winning In Life Now." She has gone on to author dozens of additional books and products in the areas of achievement, motivation, productivity and success. She owns her own publishing company and is the founder of "Book Writing Blueprint" and the "Book Bound Workshop" which helps soon-to-be authors get their story "out of their head and onto paper." Michelle knows we all have a story and is passionate about helping others tell their stories so they can impact other people's lives.

Michelle began her sales career working for Zig Ziglar right out of college. With her solid foundation in personal growth, productivity and leadership, Michelle was able to achieve extraordinary results and numerous awards, making her an in-demand sales and marketing professional. She decided to take that knowledge and start her own company to fulfill her passion of motivating, inspiring and encouraging others to live phenomenal lives. She does this through her speaking, coaching and training. Her life came full circle when she was asked to become a Ziglar Motivational Speaker representing the values and company that ignited her passion and kick-started her career back in her twenties. Michelle most recently became a Ziglar Legacy Trainer and is even more committed to carrying on the legacy of the late Zig Ziglar than ever before.

As "America's Productivity Coach," Michelle has learned the secret to overcoming procrastination and living a happier, more abundant life. She is on a mission to show audiences worldwide that they too can stop juggling, overcome procrastination, and get more done in less time in business, leadership and life!

Michelle Prince
CEO, Prince Performance Group
  & Performance Publishing
Best-Selling Author
Zig Ziglar Motivational Speaker
6841 Virginia Pkwy, Suite 103#124
McKinney, TX 75071
972-529-9743
Info@PrincePerformance.com
http://www.MichellePrince.com

CPSIA information can be obtained
at www.ICGtesting.com
Printed in the USA
BVHW040537040319
541679BV00002B/2/P